Garry Chapman

eXtreme SPORTS

AIR

WARNING:

Extreme sports can be very dangerous. Mishaps can result in death or serious injury. Seek expert advice before attempting any of the stunts you read about in this book.

This book is for my daughter Tess.

This edition first published in 2002 in the United States of America by Chelsea House Publishers, a subsidiary of Haights Cross Communications.

Chelsea House Publishers
1974 Sproul Road, Suite 400
Broomall, PA 19008-0914

The Chelsea House world wide web address is www.chelseahouse.com

Library of Congress Cataloging-in-Publication Data Applied for.

ISBN 0-7910-6609-6

First published in 2001 by
Macmillan Education Australia Pty Ltd
627 Chapel Street, South Yarra, Australia, 3141

Copyright © Garry Chapman 2001

Edited by Renée Otmar, Otmar Miller Consultancy Pty Ltd
Text design by if design
Cover design by if design
Printed in China

Acknowledgements
The author and the publisher are grateful to the following for permission to reproduce copyright material:

Cover photo of skysurfer courtesy of Photolibrary.com/Tony Stone.

Allsport/Vandystadt, pp. 20–21; Australian Picture Library/Corbis, pp. 11, 25, 27; Australian Picture Library/Vandystadt, p. 13; Coo-ee Historical Picture Library, p. 4; Getty Images, pp. 8, 15, 18–19, 29; Mary Evans Picture Library, p. 23; PhotoDisc, pp. 28, 30; Sport. The Library/Aerial Focus, p. 9; Sport. The Library/Chris McLennan, p. 14; Sport. The Library/Jeff Crow, pp. 5, 7 (insert), 26; Sport. The Library/Mark Hay, pp. 6–7; Sport. The Library/Mike Timewell, p. 10; Sport. The Library/Oioer Givois, p. 22; Sport. The Library/Tom Sanders, p. 12; Sport. The Library/Uli Wiesmeter, p. 19 (insert); Sport. The Library/Wendy Smith, pp. 16–17; Sporting Images, p. 24.

While every care has been taken to trace and acknowledge copyright the publishers tender their apologies for any accidental infringement where copyright has proved untraceable.

Contents

FLYING AS A SPORT

Orville Wright, after a catapult launch, skims through the air at Kitty Hawk in North Carolina, United States, and makes history.

The desire to fly

For thousands of years, humans have looked to the skies and wished they could fly like the birds. The ancient Greeks told stories of people who could fly. One legend told of Daedalus and his son Icarus, who attached feathers to their arms with wax and took winged flight from their island prison. When Icarus flew too close to the sun, it melted the wax and he tumbled down into the sea and drowned. The Greek god Hermes had wings attached to his feet so that he could swiftly bear messages from the gods.

WINGS LIKE A BIRD

It seemed that the only way for humans to fly was to have wings like a bird. In 1060 AD, a monk named Eilmer strapped wings to his arms and legs, and jumped from the top of his monastery tower. He crashed to the ground and was seriously injured. In the late 15th century, Italian artist and inventor Leonardo da Vinci took the dream of human-powered flight one step closer to reality. He designed a flying machine.

The first hang glider

In the 1890s, Germany's Otto Lilienthal built the first hang gliders from canvas and willow. He launched himself from an 11-meter (36 foot) high mound and made many short flights. He was killed in a crash when a gust of wind forced his glider down.

The Wright brothers

In 1903, brothers Orville and Wilbur Wright created history when their Flyer took off, flew briefly under the pilot's control, and landed safely. In the decades that followed, aircraft technology rapidly evolved. Humans had finally learned how to fly.

TAKING FLYING TO EXTREMES

Early aviators

Early **aviators** were courageous people. Often they would put their lives at great risk in the pursuit of new boundaries of flight. Some pioneered new routes across vast oceans. Others flew to the extremes of the Earth, visiting the Poles and other remote, barren places.

Spirit of adventure

The spirit of adventure never strayed far away from human flight throughout the 1900s. Modern military aircraft are capable of flying faster than the speed of sound. Stunt teams perform spectacular aerial maneuvers at air shows. Spacecraft have taken astronauts to the surface of the moon.

Parachuting

New means of taking to the skies have evolved. These new ways of flying are purely for fun. Parachuting was once a serious business. During World War II, thousands of paratroopers floated down from the sky to infiltrate enemy lines. Today, skysurfers and freestyle skydivers take parachuting to another dimension. They drop thousands of feet in **freefall**, performing incredible aerial stunts as they hurtle towards the ground.

Hang gliding

Hang gliding has come a long way since Lilienthal's crude attempts at flight. Today's hang glider pilots leap off mountain ledges and swoop and soar for hours in the **thermal** air currents that rise from the valleys below.

Bungee jumping provides adventure seekers with the ultimate thrill.

Xtreme Fact

Hot air ballooning is a very popular pastime. The air inside the balloon, heated by a propane gas burner, causes the balloon to rise. When it rises to high *altitudes*, the surrounding cold temperature cools the air inside the balloon and it loses altitude. Another blast of heat will cause the balloon to rise once again.

Bungee jumping

Bungee jumping has also taken off in a big way. People attach themselves to elastic cords and leap from bridges and other structures. The cords reach their full stretch when the jumpers are only inches from the ground, before jerking them back into the sky once more on the **rebound**. The **adrenaline rush** is huge.

Conditions for Aerial Sports

Skydiving at night can be an exhilarating experience, providing the skies are clear.

Skydiving from 4,000 meters

Extreme aerial sports take place around the world in a wide range of locations and conditions. Small planes carry **freeflying** skydivers to altitudes of around 4,000 meters (13,125 feet). As they pass over the **drop zone**, the skydivers leap from the plane to begin the breathtaking descent to the ground. During the next 60 seconds or so they will freefall through the air at speeds approaching 300 kilometers (186 miles) per hour!

Hazardous clouds

Freeflying skydivers jump in pairs. A freestylist or skysurfer is always accompanied by a camera flyer, who records the aerial stunts on video. Both skydivers must remain fully aware of each other's whereabouts at all times. Obviously, an accidental mid-air collision between the two could have disastrous consequences. Therefore, jumping in cloudy conditions can be quite hazardous. In addition to obscuring skydivers' vision of each other, clouds create other problems. They can cause goggles and **altimeters** to fog up, making it difficult for skydivers to judge their distance above the ground.

Night jumps

Some skydivers enjoy jumping at night. Night jumps are probably as safe as day jumps. However, it is important that the skies are clear enough to allow an unobstructed view of the guiding lights surrounding the drop zone.

Upwardly moving air

Hang gliders are carried up whenever they encounter areas of upwardly moving air. Hang glider pilots must develop the ability to find these upward drafts and use this rising air to keep the craft airborne for the duration of the flight. It is generally accepted that ideal conditions for hang gliding require winds ranging from zero to 50 kilometers (32 miles) per hour.

Xtreme Fact

Freeflyers freefall at speeds of around 300 kilometers (186 miles) per hour. This is much faster than skydivers who use traditional methods. Falling at such a rapid rate makes it necessary to *deploy* the *canopy* at an altitude of around 1,200 meters (4,000 feet), in order to ensure a safe landing.

Bungee jumpers take the plunge from the Kawarau Bridge, New Zealand. The first commercial bungee jumping operation started from this bridge in 1987.

Ridge lift

There are two common sources of upward air, ridge lift and thermal lift. Ridge lift occurs when the wind is travelling horizontally over the ground, then hits an obstruction such as a ridge. The ridge deflects the air upwards. There is generally a band of rising air above such a ridge, and a glider can soar back and forth within this zone.

Thermal lift

Thermal lift occurs over land that is heated by the sun. As the land heats up, it heats the air immediately above it. This rising column of warm air is known as a thermal. Thermals often begin in the valleys at the feet of mountains. Hang glider pilots launch from high cliffs and circle for hours in and around the rising currents of warm air. Whenever they sail back into the thermal, their glider is lifted to higher altitudes.

Kitty Hawk

In an interesting twist of history, a popular place for hang gliding in the United States of America is over the sand dunes at Kitty Hawk, in North Carolina. It was here in 1903 that the Wright brothers first flew a human-made craft, which they named *Kitty Hawk*.

The bungee

The first Westerners to bungee jump were members of the Oxford University Dangerous Sports Club. They jumped 75 meters (246 feet) from a bridge in Bristol, England. They then travelled to the United States, where they leapt from San Francisco's Golden Gate Bridge. When the world's first commercial bungee jumping operation started up in Queenstown, New Zealand, it too was from a high bridge. Today, bungee jumpers continue to leap from bridges, as well as from specially constructed towers.

Gear
Up for the AiR

CHOOSE YOUR JUMPSUIT

The freeflying disciplines of skysurfing and freestyle skydiving require specialized jumpsuits that differ slightly from the **jumpsuits** worn by regular **belly-to-earth** skydivers. Most freefly jumpsuits are custom-made to suit individual body shapes. They are usually made from durable, abrasion-proof fabric which does not limit movement or flap about unnecessarily. It is also essential that the jumpsuit permits unrestricted access to the handles that release the parachute.

Triangle-shaped 'wings' can be added to jumpsuits to help slow the rate of the fall.

INCREASE THE AMOUNT OF DRAG

In order to increase the amount of drag on the arms, triangle-shaped 'wings' can be added to the jumpsuit. The wings are attached to the armpits of the suit, and stretch from the wrist to the waist. When the arms are stretched out, the wings become rigid and catch the air, which helps to slow the rate of the fall.

CONTROL THE DIVE

In freestyle skydiving, clothing that allows adequate arm movement for the different stunt moves performed in freefall is needed. Suitable jumpsuits often have loose-fitting sleeves to add **drag** to arms so the dive can be controlled. Drag allows freeflyers to adjust the rate at which they are falling. This is vital, because the freestylist and the camera flyer must always remain close to each other throughout the dive.

REDUCE UNWANTED DRAG

The legs of the jumpsuit need to be skintight, so that there is minimal drag on this part of the body. The tight-fitting Velcro ankle cuffs and wrist cuffs of the suit ensure that the legs and sleeves do not catch air and ride up. This creates unwanted drag and flutter.

CREATE FREEDOM OF MOVEMENT

Warm clothing is not always required for hang gliding. Many pilots fly at low altitudes, where temperatures remain moderate. Regardless of the temperature, wear clothes that allow the freedom of movement the sport demands. Applying sunscreen provides protection against the sun's burning rays.

GLOSSARY

jumpsuits – clothing specially designed for skydiving; the freeflying jumpsuit usually has a lightweight body with arms and legs made from a heavier cotton to create 'drag' during freefall

belly-to-earth – a horizontal, face-down body position often used by traditional skydivers in freefall

drag – the amount of air resistance experienced by a skydiver

hypothermia – a medical condition caused by the lowering of body temperature to dangerous levels

DRESS FOR THE CONDITIONS

There is no specific style of protective clothing required for hang gliding or bungee jumping. Dress to suit the conditions. For high altitude flights, suitable clothing is needed to protect against the very cold temperatures. Soaring to heights of over 3,500 meters (11,500 feet) increases the risk of **hypothermia** if the body is not kept warm. Thermal undergarments provide warmth and flexibility.

Freestyle skydivers who perform head-down stunts may need looser fabric on the legs of their jumpsuits to increase the amount of drag on their legs. Helmets are essential.

DRESS DIFFERENTLY FOR HEAD-DOWN STUNTS

If a lot of head-down stunts are performed in freestyle skydiving, looser fabric on the legs of the jumpsuit, to increase the amount of drag on the legs may be needed. This gives greater balance, and allows the legs to control movement in the air. A hard helmet is essential to protect against injury during bumpy landings.

CHECK FOR SAFETY

Pay careful attention to safety when taking part in any aerial extreme sport. Make sure equipment is checked thoroughly before launching into the air. This rule also applies to the checking of harnesses, canopies and bungee cords. The consequences of not dressing appropriately for aerial sports can be disastrous.

Safety in the Air

Understand the safety routines

Despite the obvious risks involved in jumping from a plane 4,000 meters (13,125 feet) above the ground, very few freeflyers come to harm while jumping. They understand the importance of strictly sticking to the established safety routines that govern their sport.

It is very important to be aware of your altitude during freefall and before and after every move.

Be aware of your altitude

Altitude awareness is especially important for freestyle skydivers. Many three-dimensional aerial stunts use up valuable time and altitude. Vertical body shapes such as the standup or head-down positions also cause you to fall much faster than regular belly-to-earth skydiving. You may be so involved in performing your stunt that for a moment your attention moves away from the rapidly approaching ground. Make it a habit to check both the ground and your altimeters before and after every move.

Use your altimeters

Altimeters inform you of your height above the ground. They alert you when it is time to deploy the canopy. Skydivers usually refer to two altimeters: a visual one and an audible one. The visual altimeter is worn on your wrist, where it can be seen easily throughout the freefall. The audible altimeter beeps loudly when you reach the altitude where your canopy must be deployed.

AUTOMATIC ACTIVATION DEVICE

If you were to lose consciousness for a moment during the freefall, a highly accurate altimeter becomes a lifesaver. This altimeter is known as an automatic activation device. When this device detects that you are falling at **terminal velocity** too close to the ground, the reserve parachute automatically deploys. Without the assistance of this special safety device, you risk almost certain death should anything go wrong with the deployment of your main canopy.

Bungee jumping is one of the safest of the extreme sports.

Observe hang gliding safety rules

Hang gliding is a very safe sport when safety precautions are observed. Modern-day hang gliders have benefited from high-tech design improvements. They are equipped with a number of safety devices, including altimeters and reserve parachutes. Safety authorities put gliders through a series of rigorous tests before they are declared airworthy. You are weighed so that you can be matched with a glider strong enough to carry you safely **aloft**.

Ensure you know the basics

Learning the basics is another way to ensure your safety. These include:

- ☞ **skill in the basic freefall actions of turning, looping and rolling**
- ☞ **ability to start and stop spins and turns**
- ☞ **ability to recover from any loss of control**
- ☞ **constant awareness of the position of the other member of the freeflying team.**

Check your gear

The most important safety task of all is to check all equipment thoroughly before every jump. The canopy must be folded carefully and packed properly into its container, so that the lines do not become tangled. In addition to the main chute, a reserve canopy should also be packed and ready. It can be deployed immediately if the main chute fails to open.

Understand the bungee stretch

Bungee jumping is also one of the safest of the extreme sports. Human error, rather than equipment failure, has been responsible for the few bungee jumping accidents that have occurred. The key to safe bungee jumping is to understand the stretch of the cords, the distance of the fall and the weight of the jumper. Jump operators accurately measure each of these variables, and apply a mathematical formula to calculate the length of the bungee cord required.

A FORM OF SKYDIVING

For many years the cutting edge of the sport of skydiving revolved around **relative work**, which means horizontal belly-to-earth diving. One of the highlights of this form of skydiving was where teams of parachutists linked up high above the ground in neat formations.

Adrenaline rush

The biggest adrenaline rush in skydiving comes from freeflying. Freeflying refers to those disciplines of the sport that feature different body positions to the slower, traditional modes of belly-down skydiving. Two of the most popular forms of freeflying are skysurfing and freestyle skydiving.

Aerial stunts

Skysurfing and freestyle skydiving are very similar. In both sports, teams of two skydivers jump together. One performs spectacular aerial stunts during the 60 seconds or so of freefall time available. The other team member, known as the camera flyer, records the performance on video. This not only allows competition judges and the skydivers themselves to review the performance on the ground, but also brings an eager television audience right in close for all the action.

Skysurfing

During freefall, the skysurfer rides a specially designed skyboard, similar to the snowboard. The stunts performed include spinning, sliding, twisting and carving through the sky. The freestyle skydiver performs graceful gymnastic style moves as they dive through freefall at speeds approaching 300 kilometers (186 miles) per hour.

A team of freeflying skydivers takes off from a hot air balloon. The camera is positioned on the helmet of the camera flyer.

Three-dimensional flying

Freeflying is also referred to as 3D, or three-dimensional flying, because the diver has the freedom to fly with their body in any orientation, direction or speed. Freefall is the only sport where you are able to fly your body up or down, left or right, and forwards or backwards at varying speeds.

FREEFLYING

Xtreme Fact

Modern freeflying rigs use simple, dual-action systems to cope with emergencies in freefall. One handle cuts away a malfunctioning canopy, while the other rapidly deploys a reserve chute.

Learning to freefly

When learning any form of freeflying, first acquaint yourself with the slower flying positions. Once you are able to control changes in speed and direction, and are able to judge how close you are to the ground during different parts of the freefall, you are ready to move on to some of the more spectacular stunts performed by the experts.

Using the canopy

Safety is always most important. In skydiving you have to depend on the accuracy of your altimeters and the dependability of your canopy to bring yourself safely to the ground after each jump. Modern high-performance canopies are either rectangular or elliptical in shape. Canopies vary in size, depending mainly on your weight. They are remarkably stable in the air, and allow you to effectively change direction and bring about soft landings.

Synchronizing the flight

During freefall the camera flyer maneuvers around the stunt flyer to record the flight. As a team you must synchronize your flights so that you fall at the same rate. In competition, points are awarded for both the quality of the aerial tricks and the quality of the camera work. The camera flyer has to keep the stunt flyer in full view of the lens at all times. This is never easy, especially when both skydivers are freefalling at such high speeds and have just one minute to complete the entire performance!

A freeflyer exits the plane to begin freefall over the drop zone.

Staying clear of each other

Stay clear of the airspace of your partner. An accidental collision in freefall could send one or both of you spinning out of control, or may even cause one to lose consciousness.

The first skysurfers used styrofoam boogie boards. This surfer is also wearing diving flippers. The wrist altimeter lets him know how far he is from the ground.

A new freeflying sport is born

There was a time when skydivers discovered that stretching out in horizontal body positions allowed them to move around in freefall with some control over their direction. From this, the idea developed that freefalling with a flat surface could add a new element of excitement to the sport. The concept of skysurfing was born.

Experimentation

A small group of Californian skydivers first attempted to skysurf in 1980, with limited success. They jumped with styrofoam boogie boards and lay flat on them during freefall. Seven years later, Joël Cruciani became the first skysurfer to stand up on a board in the traditional surfing stance. He attached a regular surfboard to his feet, using snowboard bindings.

Cut-away bindings

French skydiver Laurent Bouquet experimented with a board similar in size to a skateboard. It was much smaller and easier to control than the surfboard used by Cruciani. In 1989, the design was improved by the addition of a binding cut-away system. This allowed the skydiver to release the board just before landing. It was also useful as a safety measure if the skydiver got into difficulty during freefall. By 1990, the skyboard had evolved to closely resemble a snowboard.

Television audiences

In 1990, the first world freestyle jump titles were held in Texas in the United States. Skysurfing featured as a demonstration sport. Pete McKeeman proposed the idea that skysurfing should be a team sport involving both a skysurfer and a camera flyer. McKeeman's goal was to create a form of skydiving that would appeal to television audiences. Within months, television commercials in Japan and Australia brought spectacular skysurfing action to the attention of millions of viewers.

Skysurfing

Coordination of moves between both members of a skysurfing team is essential.

Xtreme Fact

At the X Games in 1998, Swiss skysurfer Viviane Wegrath became the first woman to win a skysurfing medal while competing against men. Although a professional skysurfer, Wegrath also finds time to work as a ski instructor. She is also a very competent ocean surfer.

Skysurfing rules

In 1993, the first rules for competitive skysurfing were introduced. The rules cover aspects of both performance and safety, including sequences of maneuvers to be attempted, requirements for video recording, and safety standards for equipment. At around this time, a number of skydivers switched to skysurfing for the first time. They began to experiment with a variety of different freefall stunts. Many of these stunts were based on similar moves from established sports such as gymnastics, acrobatics and ice skating.

Competitive skysurfing

Competitive skysurfing consists of a series of ten skydives. In some of these dives the skysurfer must perform compulsory routines predetermined by the judges. In the remaining dives, the skysurfer is free to perform routines of their choice. Judges score each routine after viewing the video footage shot by the camera flyer. They award points for:

- ☞ degree of difficulty of each maneuver
- ☞ precision with which each move is executed
- ☞ creativity displayed during the routine
- ☞ quality of the camera work.

Skysurfers are expected to perform movements in all three dimensions during freefall.

A good team in action

It is awesome to watch a good team in action. Both flyers spin and flip and roll in unison as they hurtle through the air towards the ground. The degree of coordination between them is remarkable. As the freefall comes to an end, the camera flyer maneuvers away, and both skydivers deploy their canopies. They glide gracefully to the earth, in stark contrast to the breathtaking, rapid descent of freefall. Just a few yards above the ground, the surfer releases the board, and both flyers land gently on their feet as their canopies lightly collapse behind them.

RIDING THE AIR WAVES

As the light plane climbs to an altitude of 4,000 meters, it slowly circles over the drop zone. Both members of your skysurfing team wait by the open door for the pilot to call 'Jump run!' At this signal, your camera flyer crawls out along the plane's wing strut and hangs on there until you are ready to jump. On the count of 'three', your team jumps together.

Breathtaking view

The view from this altitude is breathtaking. Vast expanses of land extend to distant horizons in all directions. Roads, railway lines and rivers appear as thin ribbons across the terrain. Buildings and trees are tiny dots. The drop zone is clear of all obstructions, and momentarily becomes the focus of your attention as you take in your bearings and begin the freefall.

Skysurfers use a specially designed board similar to a skateboard but with snowboard-style bindings that can be released before landing.

A series of acrobatic stunts

The wind tugs relentlessly as you push your feet hard against the skyboard and stretch both arms wide to gain balance. Within seconds of leaving the plane, you are standing on the board. Using both arms to control the rate of the freefall and to initiate the aerial maneuvers, you perform a series of acrobatic stunts. Using every opportunity to explore the three dimensions of the surrounding air, you change from one body position to another with smooth transitions. At times you deliberately track away from your camera flyer, then turn back and fly past the lens, performing a new trick.

Xtreme Fact

One of the most spectacular skyboard stunts is the helicopter spin. You perform this stunt by spinning while upside down. The spinning skyboard resembles a helicopter blade.

Ten jumps a day

Once you have completed the jump, you gather the canopies and thoroughly check them. Next you repack them into the containers that hold both the main and reserve chutes. Soon, you are aboard the aircraft once again, and are heading back to 4,000 meters for your next jump. Each jump is spaced about 40 to 60 minutes apart. On a good day, a skysurfing team might average about ten jumps.

Limited training opportunities

Ten jumps a day might seem quite a lot, but this is equal to a total of only ten minutes of freefall time. Assuming that most skysurfers can find time to jump on only one day of each week, you spend only about ten minutes a week putting your skills to the test. There are very few other sports where elite athletes can train for only such a short period of time. Skysurfing teams generally practice their maneuvers and safety procedures on the ground prior to jumping.

Carving on the wind

It is great fun riding the air waves, carving on the wind. In this environment there are no limits to the body positions you can attempt. You launch into a series of full twisting **layouts** with the grace of a champion gymnast. Each brilliant stunt is captured on tape by the camera flyer alongside you. Between each maneuver, you each quickly glance at your wrist altimeters and the approaching ground. This is critical. If you miss the exact moment to stop your freefall and deploy your canopy, the consequences could be fatal.

ANOTHER FORM OF FREEFLYING

Freestyle skydiving is another form of freeflying. As with skysurfing, freestyle skydivers jump in pairs. One performs the stunts in freefall while the other records all the action with a helmet-mounted video camera. Competitive freestyle skydiving is also structured along similar lines to skysurfing. Competitors are scored over a series of ten jumps, some of which feature compulsory routines. The camera flyer's performance is rated and included in the team score, along with points awarded for the aerial stunts.

Gymnastics routine

Freestyle skydiving teams jump from altitudes of around 4,000 meters, and spend up to 60 seconds in freefall. During this time the stunt flyer uses every part of the surrounding space to perform a gymnastic routine of perfectly executed twists, spins, somersaults and poses, at speeds varying from 200 to 300 kilometers per hour. It is quite a magical sight to behold.

New tricks evolve

The three-dimensional environment in which you perform is so different to being on the ground that freestyle stunts can only be practiced in true freefall. This makes training difficult, but leads to totally new tricks evolving during the actual jumps.

Coordination between flyers

Your 60 seconds of freefall requires a focus on the perfect execution of each stunt. It also requires that you are always aware of the camera flyer's position and the time remaining until deployment. You can assist the performance by holding simple poses for the camera. Perfect coordination between the two flyers can be seen on the video tape if you remain in the center of frame and perform all tricks about this central point.

Freestyle skydiving stunts can only be practiced in true freefall.

FREESTYLE SKYDIVING

◁ 18 ▷

Gear check

Freestyle skydiving can be a perfectly safe activity if you observe the safety routines that govern the sport. Perhaps the most important safety consideration is the selection and maintenance of proper gear, including jumpsuit, canopy, harness, altimeters and release systems. Carefully fold and pack your canopy, and inspect all gear before each jump. Before exiting the plane, once again check the handles that deploy the canopy. This simple procedure could save your life.

The harness

Since you perform stunts in many different body positions, it is vital that your harness is a good fit. The harness holds in place the container with both main and reserve canopies, as well as the cut-away handles and reserve ripcords used to deploy the chutes. A poorly fitting harness may interfere with your performance. It could also cause the deployment handles to shift position. This makes it difficult to find the handles at the completion of freefall.

A growing sport

The first international freestyle skydiving competition took place in 1990 in Texas, in the United States. Television coverage of the new sport on extreme sports programs proved popular. Skydivers with years of experience in traditional, relative-work flying liked what they saw. Many were eager to take on the challenge of freestyle. By the mid-1990s, teams from more than twenty different countries were competing in major international events.

Dale Stuart

One of the world's best freestyle skydivers is Dale Stuart. For over half a decade, she won gold medals in every freestyle event she entered, including a number of world titles. Stuart introduced hundreds of new maneuvers and routines to the sport.

Xtreme Fact

Australians Ashley Crick and Jon King became world freestyle skydiving champions in October 1999. Crick, who averages about 600 jumps per year, had only been skydiving for three years.

Anyone who participates in aerial sports relies heavily on a proper system of harness and canopy. It can mean the difference between life and death when freefalling from heights of around 4,000 meters.

FREESTYLE STUNTS

Most freestyle skydivers graduate from traditional belly-to-earth flying. In order to do this, they must learn to feel comfortable at greater freefall speeds and in a variety of different body positions.

Freestyle skydivers often perform gymnastics routines. This man is in the standup position.

Try a few simple moves

One method of achieving this is to exit the plane on your back. Hold this position until you reach terminal velocity, the rate of descent at which a body can go no faster. At this time, stretch out both arms and legs, and move them around. When this feels comfortable, try a few moves similar to swimming strokes, such as backstroke and sidestroke. A couple of half rolls might complete the warm-up procedure.

Learn the standup position

Once you feel at ease moving around in three dimensions, it is time to begin with a few basic freestyle maneuvers. The standup position is a basic move which can also be used as the starting point for other tricks. The standup involves flying with your torso in a vertical position, using just your arms and legs for balance. Freefall is rapid in this position. Some flyers describe it as feeling like they are falling straight down a tube.

The standup begins in a belly-down position. Push forward lightly with your arms and make sure both legs are tucked up underneath you. Straighten both knees and firmly push your feet down into the wind. As your legs become vertical, bring the rest of your body up straight and spread both arms wide for balance.

Now try the tee

Another useful position is the tee, so named because your body forms a letter T shape. This is a very graceful, balanced freefall position. Begin belly-down, then bring one knee directly under your hip. When the foot of this leg is balanced alongside the opposite knee, straighten the leg directly downward until it is vertical. Hold this leg firm to resist wind pressure.

Progress to the layout back loop

The layout back loop begins by bringing both legs forward and down from the belly-down posture, as though you are moving into the standup position. At this point, stretch out both arms and lift your torso. As your body straightens at the waist, the wind catches your legs and flips you backwards. With your arms spread wide in the layout position, you can rotate backwards through a number of elegant loops before using your arms to stop in either a belly-down or tee position.

Fly head down

Some of the more exciting body positions involve head-down flying. You barrel towards the earth at maximum terminal velocity, in a very streamlined shape. When flying head down, it is your legs, rather than your arms, which can be used to gain balance and control.

Fun flying: the monkey
rides the pony.

Perform freestyle variations

You can perform variations of most freestyle
maneuvers by changing your arm and leg
positions. Sometimes this helps when you are
making the transition from one move to another.
Regulate your speed by using your arms to create
drag, or by presenting a less streamlined body
shape to the wind. Control your turns by twisting
your body in the desired direction.

Xtreme Fact

A non-competitive form of freestyle
skydiving is called 'fun flying'. The
rodeo dive is a fun flying stunt. One
flyer is the 'monkey' and the other
is the 'pony'. The monkey's legs are
wrapped around the pony's waist as
the monkey 'rides' astride the
pony's back during freefall.

UNASSISTED HUMAN FLIGHT

Hang gliding ultimately gave humans the ability to fly like a bird. It remains the only true means of unassisted human flight.

Modern hang gliders use the latest technology to provide the glider pilot with the easiest possible flight.

Francis Rogallo

Today's hang glider can trace its development to Francis Rogallo. He worked for the United States space agency, NASA, as a research scientist. Rogallo's aim was to develop a non-rigid flying machine. His work over several decades led to the development of a flexible wing glider. In 1962, Rogallo's idea was put forward as a possible means of returning the *Gemini* spacecraft to Earth without the aid of a parachute.

John Dickenson

The following year, Australian John Dickenson saw illustrations of the *Gemini* and the Rogallo Wing in a magazine. He began making model gliders based directly on the flexible wing principle. Within six months, Dickenson had his first hang glider in the air, having been towed behind a boat until it was airborne. It was constructed of wood, aluminum and iron with plastic sheeting. Dickenson's original Ski Wing glider was built at a total cost of 24 Australian dollars (US$13.30).

Design improvements

Throughout the late 1960s, Dickenson continued to improve on his design until it was capable of reaching high altitudes and staying aloft for several hours at a time. By the early 1970s, enthusiasts in California had begun experimenting with different glider designs, including one constructed from polythene and bamboo. Design developments led to hang gliders that were easier to fly and harder to crash. Throughout the 1970s, the sport benefited from a huge boost in popularity.

High-tech design

Modern hang gliders use the latest technology to take full advantage of lighter, stronger materials. They feature aircraft-quality aluminum and stainless steel construction, with tough Dacron sails. A series of wires holds the structure stable. Hang gliders vary in weight, depending on the weight of the individual pilot. Most are capable of carrying quite substantial loads.

Decision-making ability

Hang gliding is a sport with wide appeal. Pilots can range from adolescents to senior citizens. You do not require great strength to fly the craft, simply the ability to make decisions based on safety considerations, and the skill to implement those decisions when they are made. Staying aloft and having fun relies on balance and endurance.

High-altitude flying

High-altitude flights can last for several hours. You may soar to heights of well over 3,000 meters (9,840 feet). At this altitude it can be very cold, so you need to dress accordingly to stay warm. As a general rule, air temperature usually drops by about 6 degrees Celsius for every 1,000 meters (3,280 feet) of altitude. Hang gliders have been flown successfully in freezing, sub-zero temperatures.

Larry Tudor

In 1985, Larry Tudor established a world record for altitude when he flew his glider to a height of 4,343.4 meters (14,250 feet) over Lone Pine, California. Tudor also set world distance records for glider flight. In 1990, he flew a total of 488.2 kilometers (303 miles) in a straight line from New Mexico to Kansas in the United States. Two years earlier he had set the record for the longest out and return flight. He covered a total distance of 310.3 kilometers (193 miles) on a flight from Lone Pine, California.

Xtreme Fact

Paragliding is a sport closely related to hang gliding. Courageous pilots launch from cliffs and glide around in the thermal air currents, using canopies similar to those used by skydivers.

Solo Flight

Most people learn to hang glide using tandem training techniques. This involves flying with a qualified instructor who demonstrates maneuvers and gives you a feel for the sport while still maintaining control of the craft. With proper training, solo flight is soon a reality.

Most people learn to hang glide in tandem with a qualified instructor.

Take off

You begin your flight by wedging the glider onto your shoulders, lifting it and proceeding to the start of the launch ramp. Hang gliders can be launched into the wind from any reasonably steep slope, providing you can generate sufficient take-off speed. Accelerate down the ramp and launch into the air. The feeling is magical as the wind lifts the glider and carries it safely clear of the ridge.

Seek out rising air

Once you are airborne, seek out zones of upward-rising air. Rising air is created when the wind passes over a ridge and is deflected upward, or when air heated by the land rises in columns known as thermals. The thermals lift the glider, sometimes by as much as 900 meters (3,000 feet). Once in the column of rising air you can skillfully maneuver the craft as it soars, swoops and carves turns through the sky.

Control the glider

You are suspended by a strap connected to the glider's frame, which is why the sport is named 'hang gliding'. Control the glider with subtle shifts of your body, forwards and backwards and from side to side at the end of the strap. Each body movement shifts the center of gravity and causes the craft to turn in your intended direction.

Control your air speed

You also need to control the air speed of the hang glider, regardless of the wind speed. Use small shifts of body weight to do this. Each maneuver takes some time to master, but gradually you will develop a deft touch for controlling every motion of the glider.

Perform aerial stunts

Not all hang glider pilots are satisfied with simply gliding around on gentle currents of air. A rapidly growing extreme form of the sport is stunt flying. Expert stunt pilots use specially constructed hang gliders to perform a wide variety of gravity defying aerial tricks. Some of their spinning barrel rolls and upside-down maneuvers are simply stunning to watch.

Land safely

After an hour or more of soaring high over the surrounding countryside, you look in the direction of the landing field. By watching the movement of objects fluttering in the breeze, you will be able to determine the wind direction at ground level. You need an area of about 15 by 60 meters (50 by 200 feet) of flat, clear ground to land the glider. Skillfully maneuvering the glider into the wind, lightly touch down and land smoothly on both feet.

Towed for take off

Solo flights are possible even in places where there is no slope available for launch. Hang gliders can be towed into the air by a number of different means. Some of the commonly used methods of towing gliders include the use of speedboats, trucks, winches and ultralight aircraft. Once the glider reaches the appropriate height and speed, you activate a release device and the tow rope drops away.

Landing a hang glider can be a painful experience without skillful maneuvering.

FEEL THE FEAR

It is hard to go past bungee jumping if you want a sport that will send the adrenaline pumping through your body. It takes a great deal of courage to stand atop a high precipice and leap out into its depths. It is good to have some fear at first. This ensures that you properly consider all safety precautions before you jump. You need strong courage to overcome your initial fear.

You need courage to overcome the fear of jumping into the air from a high platform.

Fly like a bird
With arms spread wide, your body arcs out into space in a graceful dive through freefall. You fly like a bird, and the feeling is wonderful. Then gravity takes over and the descent begins. You hurtle headfirst towards the ground, at a speed approaching terminal velocity. A split second before fatal impact occurs, you are suddenly jerked back with great force by the elastic cord tied to your ankles.

Rebound
The rebound tugs you back high into the air. You launch into a series of acrobatic aerial stunts before gravity drags you down once again. This time the rebound is not as strong, but you still go high enough to perform one or two more stunts on the end of the cord.

Return to the platform
Eventually, the jump is over and you come to rest at the end of the cord. There you wait for the assistants to drop you a rope and pull you back to the platform. A pulley system is used to do this. As you peer down over the edge to where you've just been, you can feel your heart beating fast. You cannot wait to jump again!

BUNGEE JUMPING

Bungee jumping started on Pentecost Island in the South Pacific. The jumpers use vines tied to their ankles.

HISTORY OF BUNGEE JUMPING

The first records of bungee jumping can be traced to tiny Pentecost Island in the South Pacific. The Pentecost Islanders retell the ancient legend of a woman who climbed a tall tree to escape her abusive husband. When he began climbing up after her, the woman tied a vine to her ankles. As her husband lunged for her, the woman leapt from the tree and was saved by the vine. Her husband, however, plunged to his death. Impressed by her courage, the men of the island began to repeat the woman's heroic stunt.

Land diving

Each year at yam harvest time, the people of Pentecost Island build a tall tower on the side of a hill. They clear the ground of obstacles and pound the dirt beneath the jump until it is soft. The men tie vines to their ankles and dive from the tower. Remarkably, the vines pull them up just inches short of crashing into the dirt. The first Westerner to try land diving was a reporter for *National Geographic* magazine, who attempted the plunge in 1970.

Dangerous Sports Club

Members of Oxford University's Dangerous Sports Club were inspired by the land divers of Pentecost Island. This Club carried out the first organized bungee jump from the Clifton Suspension Bridge in Bristol, England in 1979. They followed this up with a series of jumps from bridges in the United States.

A.J. Hackett

In 1987, A.J. Hackett, a New Zealander, upset French authorities by bungee jumping from the Eiffel Tower in Paris. Later that year, Hackett established the world's first commercial bungee jumping operation from the Kawarau Suspension Bridge, located near Queenstown in New Zealand.

Xtreme Fact

In 1980, David Kirke, of the Oxford University Dangerous Sports Club, established a new height record. He bungee jumped from the 320-meter high (1,050 foot) Royal Gorge Bridge in Colorado, United States, using a 140-meter long (460 foot) cord.

BUNGEE VARIATIONS

Commercial bungee jumping evolved separately in New Zealand and the United States, during the late 1980s. The cord systems used in each country are vastly different.

New Zealand cord system

The New Zealand system employs a single, all-rubber cord. The cord is made up of more than 1,000 individual strands of rubber tied together. All-rubber cords stretch to approximately four times their resting length. A towel is wrapped around the jumper's ankles, and the cord is attached with nylon mesh webbing. A safety line is also attached to the jumper. The weight of the jumper is recorded and the length of the all-rubber cord is altered accordingly. This ensures that at full stretch it will stop the jumper just short of the ground.

American cord system

The United States uses a system of shock cord. This has a rubber core enclosed by a nylon sheath. Shock cord was originally developed by the military to absorb the impact of dropping heavy equipment by parachute. The cords are bundled together in a ratio determined by the weight of the jumper, one cord for every 23 kilograms (50 pounds) of weight. Usually between three and six bundled cords will be used. These cords stretch to twice their resting length. They are attached by spring-loaded protection devices known as karabiners to safety harnesses, either at the waist and shoulder or at the ankle.

Smoother, slower flight

All-rubber cords are shorter than sheathed cords because of their added stretch. Therefore, there is less freefall on the all-rubber cord before it catches and begins to slow the fall. The resulting flight is smoother and slower than that of the sheathed cord, but the rebound is considerably higher.

The New Zealand all-rubber cord system is tied around the bungee jumper's ankles.

Challenge and excitement

Bungee stunts introduce a greater degree of challenge to the sport. They also increase the level of excitement. Ankle harnesses allow greater freedom than chest and waist harnesses for head-first diving and other breathtaking aerial stunts.

Flips and twists

An endless variety of bungee stunts is possible. Flips are great fun. Front flips are performed by rotating head over heels in the direction you are facing. Back flips are similar, but the direction is reversed. Jump routines featuring multiple flips are awesome to watch. Twists can be introduced to many tricks. These are performed by rotating your body either to the left or to the right along an axis extending from head to foot. Inverted tricks are performed while the body is suspended upside down from ankle harnesses.

The pogo

Another great trick for jumpers wearing ankle harnesses is the pogo. Your body must be upright, with your feet in a standing position as the rebound begins. As you hold the cord tight you are shot back into the air, still upright, like someone bouncing on a pogo stick.

Sandbagging

Some jumpers wanted to increase the intensity and height of the rebound. They developed the practice of 'sandbagging', where you hold onto additional weights when you jump. A split second before the rebound, you release the heavy weight and are propelled back into the air with a much greater amount of energy than is normal. This often causes you to rebound higher into the air than the original take-off platform.

Xtreme Fact

In 1998, 25 people bungee jumped together from a height of 50 meters (164 feet). They performed in a mass jump from the Deutsche Bank building in Frankfurt, Germany.

Bungee jumping from a crane.

Freeflying Jargon

biff

a botched landing where the freeflyer does not land on two feet

> "I misjudged the wind coming in, and totally biffed the landing."

chicken soup

a dive routine which does not go as planned

> "I made chicken soup of that last jump."

chop

to release either the skyboard or the canopy in an emergency

> "My main chute was tangled, so I had to chop it and deploy the reserve."

dirt-dive

to practice a skydiving routine on the ground

> "My camera flyer and I went through the dirt-dive a couple of times before take-off."

DZ

drop zone

> "We made our exit as the plane circled over the DZ."

fly-by

to move away, then track back past the camera flyer while performing a stunt

> "He performed a couple of front loops while I filmed the fly-by."

jump run

the plane's final pass over the drop zone

> "On the jump run, the camera flyer was the first to exit."

Olav

to fly head first in a vertical position; named after freestylist Olav Zipser

> "She reached terminal velocity while performing an Olav."

punch a cloud

to freefall through a cloud formation — an unsafe practice

> "I'm not going to jump today. I don't like the thought of punching clouds all day."

skygod

a person with a reputation for superior freefall ability

> "I'm going to work at improving my stunts until I become a skygod."

turf surf

to skim over the ground, just inches above the surface, when coming in to land

> "He rode the canopy in beautifully, and turf surfed the last few feet before landing."

whuffo

someone who does not skydive

> "Sometimes I prefer to sit back like a whuffo and watch all the action on a television screen."

Glossary

adrenaline rush
the special feeling that accompanies a thrilling experience

aloft
in the air

altitude awareness
the ability of a skydiver to determine their distance above the ground during freefall

altimeter
a device used for recording the height of a skydiver above the ground

altitude
height above the ground

aviator
someone who flies a form of aircraft

belly-to-earth
a horizontal, face-down body position often used by traditional skydivers in freefall

canopy
a parachute

deployment
the action of releasing a canopy to slow down a skydiver in freefall

drag
the amount of air resistance experienced by a skydiver

drop zone
the area on the ground where a skydiver intends to land

freefall
that part of a dive where the skydiver falls unaided by a canopy

freeflying
any form of skydiving involving body positions other than belly-to-earth

hypothermia
a medical condition caused by the lowering of body temperature to dangerous levels

jumpsuit
clothing specially designed for skydiving; the freeflying jumpsuit usually has a lightweight body with arms and legs made from a heavier cotton to create 'drag' during freefall

layout
a gymnastic body position also performed by skydivers, featuring a slightly arched back and the arms spread wide

rebound
the action of a bungee cord as it reaches full stretch and springs back into the air

relative work
the traditional form of the sport of skydiving, horizontal belly-to-earth diving

terminal velocity
the rate of freefall at which a falling body can go no faster

thermal
a rising current of warm air

Index